If the Moon was God

Cheyenne Valkyrie

BookLeaf Publishing

Presentation by *BookLeaf Publishing*

Web: www.bookleafpub.com

E-mail: info@bookleafpub.com

ISBN: 9789358310306

First edition 2023

This Is How It Ends

There is an ocean in my belly and the tide is
high tonight.
The Moon pulls the words straight up from my
throat:
You have to stop mourning everything.

We sit here in tandem, breathing and
remembering, and while endings are never easy
I cannot help but smile. If I stood up right now
and twirled back and forth I wonder if you could
hear the waves lapping up inside of me.
You reach out and touch the upturned wrist lying
in my lap and ask me:
How?

I think of meeting you so early in my life. I think
of every person I have become since then.
I think of dreams that have risen and died, of
fears and anxieties I have outgrown or grown
into. How can I tell you that it's possible to still
love someone and carry grief around inside of
you?
How can I explain that loving is a choice and
I've decided to no longer be the only one
picking it.

There is an ocean in my belly and the tide is high tonight.

This Is How It Starts

I stare at your back, where the end of your hair
meets the costal curve of your spine and think
Did you have an end before they touched you?
Or were you a series of exposed ellipses,
vertebrae of braille, begging someone to run
their fingers down to hear a message.
What soft thing do you have to say?
But I lean in and kiss your shoulder instead and
tuck away the thought of other people being
here before me.

Father's Day

They don't tell us enough that love can be violent. That she can push us up against the wall and demand we scrounge up some change. So here we are, fishing away inside of lint-filled pockets, looking for our next existential crisis. What I mean to say is when we passed by each other without speaking I felt like my ribs had suddenly become prison bars and I can't stand the silence.

What I mean to say is sometimes when I lay in bed alone I quietly count all the ways to say I'm sorry and none of them feel sufficient enough. There is a thread sticking out of my blanket now, the one that you bought me, and I've pulled and pulled until it's gone and unraveled itself. That's where I stand, with a look of grief on my face and a pile of yarn at my feet and my hands wishing they knew how to pass on the memo of apologies.

Here is my attempt I guess: I am sorry. There are a thousand different ways you can tell someone you love them, but it wasn't a language I spoke.

If Icarus was Gay

I.
From a half-cracked window, He stares out and
thinks to himself
This wasn't his idea in the first place.

II.
He looks out onto the day, and holds it quietly
on his tongue.
The light had become painful- he was dazzled
by it.
Made dizzy by this extension of space.
He thinks of all the what-ifs, all the half-formed
sentences that
died right when he began to speak, but how
ready he was.
He took a step up and suddenly, a great fear
came upon him
of all the unknowns.
Would he know how to do this?
Would he rise or fall? As if rising was somehow
the greater risk here.
Out of his fright, he stood at the edge of the
window and challenged
the whole world- nothing happened.

And suddenly he forgot to be afraid.
Fear assumed the guise of curiosity.
He never experienced the hurt of a fall before, so
There he went, stepping boldly out upon the air,
and
He fell forward.

Don't tell my Mother, but

I've gone and swallowed the Sun.
Leaned over and tipped out a bit of her glory,
Her goodness.
Drank her in as if a dog in the summer heat.

I thought she'd taste like citrus, like pulp
in the mouth; grapefruit being broken open, but
I'm
two shots deep and she tastes like
air.
And I'm a kid again, running down the street
with
ribs aching and lungs screaming: "More.
More, More, More. Fill me up, I need more."
And I'm a kid again,
greedily sucking down whatever I can get
to stop the burning:
A bit of freedom, of joy, of
rebellion dressed in a button-down and wearing
Nikes at the bar, smiling at me.

Don't tell my Mother but, I've gone and
decided to blind myself.
Stare straight at the oncoming light and touch
her,

as if the rays she gives off would refract and
we could dance in the colors.
My skin feels sunburnt and my molecules
vibrate uncontrollably, but her eyes
speak of redemption, and her lips of prayer
so I fold myself into her, swearing up and
down that, yes:
Salvation can be found when she lays her
hands on me.

I met you & realized I don't want you to see me this way

There is a house on the corner of Killam. Its
pavement is cracked from the weeds pushing
back against the tyranny of concrete and its
shutters are half-closed, paint peeling down the
sides.
Its state of being wildly swings from appearing
completely abandoned to having a crowd
spilling out onto the street.
Still, all the while, it holds a reverent kind of
silence. The kind that makes you sit in the back
corner of a church pew, chewing the inside of
your cheek, and wondering if you are a sinner.

I push on the door with broken down locks and
take a look at the state of disrepair. How many
people have come and gone, leaving their mark
on the walls and the trash on the floor.
I clamor over upturned furniture until I reach the
living room, and slowly start to clean.
One corner at a time, one room at a time, slow
and tedious.
I take breaks to breathe
I take breaks to cry

Face turned to the Sun

This is not an apology, or a break up message.
This is a missing person's poster.

You were last seen being shipped down the Nile,
and in a moment of transparency,
I was the one who pushed you off the shore.

You were wearing softness and revolution,
which is to say in modern terms:
you were wearing a hoodie and Nikes.

There is a feeling in my belly that feels
apocalyptic and the only solution
I could think of was to extract you from me as
quickly as possible

There has been no alleviation; in fact I have
fallen even more ill.
My body has turned into an earthquake and I
have thought more of your hands

In the last 3 hours than I have thought of fingers
and palms before.
The feeling of missing you is something I tried
to pluck out and

Dissect but it just whispered back to me of your
eyes
And your smile and the way your eyelashes lay
themselves on your cheek

Like birds posed to take off for flight because
I've approached too closely.
So I've been holding my breath when I look at
you ever since.

Please call me when this reaches you.

Smoke Signals

Me leaving your bed is not an act of exit but of
metaphysical displacement.
I hope you feel it when you roll over, the dent of
where my body was as it held my weight.
I hope my perfume clings to your sheets and my
hair haunts your pillow and that you know that
getting up to leave was a thing of true labor.
Peeling myself away as if extricating myself
from the deepest lake found nearby.
At the rate my love carries, feel free to call the
rescue team so I can be airlifted out; it's tied
itself around my wrists like cement blocks
attempting to pull me back under, and you roll
over and whisper "*5 more minutes*" and I realize
you wouldn't even need to push me in for me to
drown.

SEXTS

I.
We lay sprawled out in a darkened room,
Legs untucked from covers as sweat is on our
backs
Close your eyes, I whisper.
I will press so heavy on your eyelids that
darkness
will fold in on itself.
Let me show you light, let me
swallow your laughter

II.
There is circulation in my hands as they
run through the never-ending checklist of things
I would like to do to you, but I settle with
tucking your
hair behind your ear and swallowing up your
soft sighs.
Expanding with hot air and things I leave unsaid
in quiet moments until I am all
exhales, all CO2
I know they've written off climate change, but
how do I report
to the environmental studies there is a forest fire
in my belly when you touch me.

I am ravaged, there is a trail of destruction
that started at my neck and
I am unsure of how to stop it.

III.
We are archaeologists pulling back rubble,
pulling back sheets and fears and exposing
something Holy here, something demanding
reverence,
and God do you pull that out of me.
You kiss me and my lungs fall prostrate,
I forget what it's like to breathe and I am in a
cathedral, stained glass in the hues of blue and
ivory
awash me as I lay fallen off a pew, and I am
counting
every freckle you have in an attempt to best
describe you when I meet God.
"She's the one with the constellation of hope
across her face",
"She's the one with wisdom woven into her
hair"
I'm not sure how to convince Him you kiss like
a sinner
without getting jealous, so I don't. There are
parts of you
I tuck inside myself for safekeeping and I hold
my chest
and say your name as my last rites,

My lungs refuse, still, to stand.

15

Your shoe is untied

Maybe that wasn't the way to start the
conversation,
But I've been staring down at your feet trying to
formulate a way to tell you:

It's unfair. You're standing there on the remnants
of every person who has come before you
And all the things they have said, and done
I carry around with me as if a provision for war
instead of acknowledging it's more like a
pack of stray dogs, snapping at my heels
when I think of slowing down, and

Behind me is every past version of myself
killed and shed, as if I were a great serpent
on the move. As if every layer let go was my
own personal metamorphosis, but it feels
less beautiful and more like
a personal flaying.

I'm really trying to tell you I think we are
metamorphic rocks,
and it is laughable except the thought makes
me want to cry when I think of how all the time
and pressure and heat have turned us into

something else entirely.
And I'm just shedding layers and compressing
in on myself to get to the truth buried at the core:
I want you to know me, even now
when I probably couldn't even pick her out in a
crowd,
but God I want you to know me.
And every word I have buried somewhere deep
inside I'd give them to you as
an act of commitment of unabashed gratitude
that
You're standing here at all.

How I say I love you

I will rub rind into your back until
my hands are drenched in the juice
of a fruit that can only be born in sunshine,
and you will smell of its rays and rain.

Vanishing Point

You are staring at me and I am staring in turn at
the hole in my sweater that is gracing the bottom
right corner seam.

My pinky has wiggled through and I am
thinking about how I wish I could tell you all the
things I have stored up inside of me. All the
fears, all the doubts.
I wonder if you or someone you know has
Trypophobia as I'm suddenly so sure I must be
riddled with holes inside.

How do I tell you that I used to try and alleviate
all my rage that had built up by hurting myself.
Saw it as an act of bloodletting, like it was a
disease that could just flow out of me.
Or the time as a child that someone got so angry
they started to choke me, and the only grace my
cries brought me was them saying
"If you can scream you can breathe"
And I feel like I've been screaming ever since.

I look up at you and hope that all you see in me
is the person I've tried so hard to become. I want
to eek out joy from every little moment I can get

my hands on. Want them to get sticky sweet like
a kid grabbing everything in a candy store. I
want to shriek with laughter and get sick with
hope because I'm so tired of fighting off my
sadness, I've decided just to starve it instead.

My pinky is in the hole of my sweater and my
eyes are trained on you.

Freshly Squeezed

Would you like me to be poetic when I tell you I
break open like an orange?
A fingernail digging into my flesh and I am
ripped open and exposed.
Would you like me to tell you that so many
people expect warmth on their tongue when they
meet me and I'm more worried about the acidic
wear on their teeth.
How do I tell you I hold in me something
volatile? Veins stretching across soft skin that
get stuck in your smile.
My fears: organically grown and ethically
sourced, pulp in the back of your throat. Drink
me in and know that everything that follows me
will taste of citrus, of warmth, of repulsion. May
it remind you of me at all times. May it remind
you that I was cultivated and not just an
accident.
May it remind you that the soil and water that
helped grow me were by the World's hands and
never Man.
Never Man.

Fluorescent Lights

I wish you knew how much hesitancy hurts
As if love personified was a nursing home and
our rules were:
Habitual Visitations

Content to be confined, but never fully have a
defined reason for commitment.
I wonder what you tell the nurses when you
come. Are you a
Lover or a brother or a friend? Is this from a
place of responsibility, or is
this your act of remembrance?

I am not disillusioned, but I didn't think death
would be so drawn out.

I hear it now- the tell-tale signs of your shoes on
linoleum floors
And I wait until we are both sitting in silence
looking at each other,
Too afraid to pass under doors not painted by
hyssop, waiting
For the right time that never seems to come.

An Obituary of Joy

If death is an illusion I hope you saw open my
casket like a magician just to discover I'm gone.

Feel free not to look too far for me, I am now the
atmosphere.
I am the clouds coming down to kiss your ankles
like fog rolling in.
There is no ending or beginning. There is no
illusion of who I am.
I am unashamed joy filling a tense moment.
I am the rushing of laughter after an awkward
pause.
I hope more than anything when you think of me
you see small miracles.
That you will not take an inventory of losses
when I go, just stock in the Divine.

Corporate Ladder

We slink into shadows
And steal heavy-handed kisses
And trade like butcher and baker.
We are ovens of heat and fire
pushed up against shadowed walls
to hide away from the moon's light.
Pull me up into alleyways,
dark and damp stones with your
mouth on my neck, and your teeth,
in my flesh and I lost my hands
somewhere. The streetlights are making
pools of light and we are running through them
outpacing whoever might be looking. Running-
through fields of baked bread and we are
cleaving
into something or someone
that I don't entirely understand.
There is a warmth from your mouth
that is not entirely unlike an oven.
And I am crawling in to know.
And I am crawling in to be.

An Ode to Weariness

Show them your teeth.
Be charming more as a surprise than
a requirement, and hold your callous hands
that act like windshield wipers against your
cheeks
by your side, curled up so tightly that
half moons are being dug into the palms as if
You were digging holes there to plant
a small garden.

There is dirt under your fingernails and
Your knees are weak.
They ask if something is wrong, and all you give
them is lumped shoulders
and a stare that reminds them
They do not know you.
Your garden is starting to bloom, but you don't
seem to notice.

Your back aches, from
constantly bending and stretching and
contouring to fit into spaces you are not wanted
or feel like you belong. But every time you
rake your hands over your face in an attempt

to wash away the fleeting feeling of weariness
that comes, more green appears.

It's not until she holds your hand, laughs and
points out the
abundance of cherry tomatoes growing
that you finally see them there.
She helps you harvest them,
cut them up in the kitchen and put them in a
pasta salad
so you can enjoy the fruits of your labor.
She teases you for being soft enough to be a
gardener and your
hands rest gently in your lap.

The Ending

Here is my hope for you:

I hope the Universe unhinges its jaw and
swallows you whole.
Digests you unsuitably slow, like a boa
constrictor.
I hope you are confined in love, that there is an
endless amount of time and space and
all-consuming joy when you get to the pit of its
belly.

I hope that what dissolves away in the stomach
acid is all the things the world has demanded of
you. All the variations of yourself you had to
make to best fit in. May the hunk of your being
left behind be raw and honest. What is identity
anyway if it's not what we attempt to label
ourselves as we go about living.
I hope you remember at the end of your
digestive journey that you are loved and you
have loved, and that's really all there is to life.